Dec 86

CHRISTMAS

The Christmas season now is here;
Its fragrance fills the air.
Bells are ringing, carollers singing;
Love is everywhere.
For Christmas is a loving time
As shown by God's love
In sending us his only Son,
A gift from Heaven above.

The Christmas season now is here;
Its presence fills the heart.
Joy and laughter—happiness—
Are felt both near and far.
For Christmas is a happy time,
Expressed in giving-style,
So wrap and tie each Christmas gift
With a loving, cheerful smile.

Loise Pinkerton Fritz

Publisher, Patricia A. Pingry
Editor, Ramona Richards
Art Director, David Lenz
Permissions, Kathleen Gilbert
Copy Editor, Peggy Schaefer
Phototypesetter, Tammy Walsh
Production Manager, Jan Johnson

ISBN 0-8249-1048-6

IDEALS—Vol. 43, No. 8 December MCMLXXXVI IDEALS (ISSN 0019-137X) is published eight times a year,
February, March, May, June, August, September, November, December
by IDEALS PUBLISHING CORPORATION, Nelson Place at Elm Hill Pike, Nashville, Tenn. 37214-8000
Second class postage paid at Nashville, Tennessee, and additional mailing offices.
Copyright © MCMLXXXVI by IDEALS PUBLISHING CORPORATION.
POSTMASTER: Send address changes to Ideals, Post Office Box 148000, Nashville, Tenn. 37214-8000
All rights reserved. Title IDEALS registered U.S. Patent Office.
Published simultaneously in Canada.

SINGLE ISSUE—$3.50
ONE-YEAR SUBSCRIPTION—eight consecutive issues as published—$15.95
TWO-YEAR SUBSCRIPTION—sixteen consecutive issues as published—$27.95
Outside U.S.A., add $4.00 per subscription year for postage and handling.

The cover and entire contents of IDEALS are fully protected by copyright and must
not be reproduced in any manner whatsoever. Printed and bound in U.S.A.
by The Banta Co., Menasha, Wisconsin.

Front and back covers from H. Armstrong Roberts

Inside front cover by Robert Holland

Joyous Season

When the Christmas star is shining,
When the holly wreaths are hung,
Then has come the joyous season
And the Christmas songs are sung.

These are symbols of a season
That should live throughout the year,
Bringing peace and joy and gladness
And dispelling doubt and fear.

Then we hear the cheerful greetings
Of a friend who meets a friend;
May their friendly warmth and gladness
Live forever—never end.

May the joyous Christmas spirit
Live forever in each heart;
May God's love and blessed mercy
Hold each close and not depart.

Roy Z. Kemp

Photo Opposite
CHRISTMAS BRILLIANCE
Robert Cushman Hayes

Mid-Winter Melody

Craig E. Sathoff

The melody mid-winter brings
Is one of mellow tones
And fellowship around the fire
And popcorn heaped in bowls.

Though winds may blow and snow may fall,
There is a warmth inside
That fills the house with coziness
Where peace and joy abide.

Mid-winter gives us time to think,
To plan and hope and dream,
The time for taffy pulls and chess
And date cake and whipped cream.

Photo Overleaf
VERMONT WINTER SUNRISE
Fred Dole

When winds raise up a roar outside,
A cozy place to be
Is seated round the oak table
With friends and family.

Hot chocolate, songs, and laughter gay
Add splendor to the night
And form a winter melody
With harmony just right.

Season's Wishes

We pray for the Savior's blessings,
That his special guiding hand
Might touch the lives this season
Of all people of this land,
So they will know that Christmas
Is more than just a day;
It's formed of love and caring
In a very special way.

We pray that the Savior's promises
Might live through things we share,
That sparks might start from others
As his people show they care,
So Christian love will linger on
Long past the day of birth,
Till others know its meaning
All over this great earth.

Thelma A. Martin
Bremerton, WA

Christmas Morning

The hurry and worry
And dithery flurry
Of shopping and buying
And wrapping and tying,
Of wishing and seeking
And carefully peeking
And wondering what
The others have got
Are over . . . and how
Becalmed it is now.

S. H. Dewhurst
Falls Church, VA

The Evergreen Scent

You can tell it's Christmas by carols and bells,
But Christmas also has special smells:
Gingery tang from the cookie pan
Sends out word of the gingerbread man;
Cinnamon, nutmeg, cloves, and mace
Waft in clouds from the cookery place.
There's sage for dressing and chestnuts popping,
Woodsy vanilla and almond topping,
Rich dark cakes and gold mince pies
With scent so strong it waters the eyes,
And wax on floors and polish on handles,
And wintry fragrance of bayberry candles.
But the very best Christmas smell there'll be
Is the mountain-green of the Christmas tree!

Virginia Brasier
San Bernardino, CA

Reflections

Grandmother:
The Conscience of a Child

Reproving glances, stopping young hands from danger
They cannot understand.
Love in eyes filled with wisdom
And knowledge they wish to share.
Unselfish and caring with tender ones,
Never to hurt, always to love and hold.
Singing songs slightly off key
Filled with hope and pride for their grandsons.
But that is what grandmothers are.
Love in a person you always look up to.
No matter how tall you are.

Ricky Caron
Lakeland, FL

Bethlehem Night

Beneath the deep oppressing yoke of Rome
The city sleeps.
A shepherd, lost in tender thoughts of home,
His vigil keeps.
The crystal stars reach down to touch the hill
With fragile light;
A distant lullaby is heard this still,
Uncommon night.
A mother looks out from a stable door;
A world awakes, to be the same no more.

June A. Berry
Spokane, WA

Editor's Note: Readers are invited to submit unpublished, original poetry, short anecdotes, and humorous reflections on life for possible publication in future *Ideals* issues. Please send copies only; manuscripts will not be returned. Writers will receive $10 for each published submission. Send materials to "Readers' Reflections," Ideals Publishing Corporation, Nelson Place at Elm Hill Pike, Nashville, Tennessee 37214.

High on a Hill

Come walk with me to the tall, red hill
Which is now knee-deep in snow,
And see the white immaculate spread
That lies silently far below.

The bright sun casts a glimmering gleam
On the landscape soft and white;
It decks the earth with a magic cloak
That fell silently in the night.

The great trees stand tall and bare
As if the world was asleep.
They outline beauty far and near
For the world of man to reap.

The snow-white spread lies regally
Around each plant and shrub serene.
Great rocks look like pillows
That are neatly tucked behind a screen.

Standing upon the hill in awe and wonder,
We drink of the beauty given freely,
A miracle sent down from Heaven
To beauty lovers such as we!

Mamie Ozburn Odum

The Popcorn Trees

There is no Christmas tree more beautiful than one decorated by nature. After several years of little or no snowfall during the holidays, this year seemed to have us right in the middle of the snow belt. Wild winter winds bustled in between the Blue Ridge Mountains and dumped heavy snows all along our valley. The snow pirouetted into circular drifts across the meadowland, but little of the powder remained on our swaying pines, spruces, and hemlocks. Occasionally, dark charcoal clouds would roll in, depositing a wet snow upon the countryside and woodlands, dramatically changing our frozen, drab, bare villages into a dreamland. During the morning hours, the world would be a scenic panorama of diamonds glittering upon puffs of fantasy. It was breathtakingly lovely, but didn't last once the sun came out again.

While the snow neglected our outdoor trees, we concentrated on the one we had inside. On Christmas Day, the grandchildren had everyone up before dawn to gather round our Christmas tree in the living room of the farmhouse. We all agreed that it was the most perfect Christmas tree we had ever had. It was indeed a spectacular sight, perfectly shaped and handsomely decorated, and the scent of fresh pine wafted through the house. We didn't think a more beautiful tree could exist.

As daylight slowly emerged in the valley, however, we noticed that there had been a heavy snowfall during the night. The pines, hemlocks, and spruces were now decorated with adorable little plops of soft, glistening, feathery snow.

"They look as though they've been decorated with popcorn," the children decided, and we all agreed. The popcorn snow must have frozen to the limbs, for the trees were decorated with the popcorn snow throughout the holidays. This has been the only time in all of my country Christmases that I've shared in the joy of having our trees decorated with popcorn snow by the best decorator of all, Mother Nature.

Helen Colwell Oakley

Untitled painting by
David Lenz
Used by permission of
Art Pfitzinger

Christmas Eve Party Delights

Mulled Holiday Punch

Makes 14 servings

1 48-ounce can pineapple-pink grapefruit juice
4 cups cranberry juice
1 cup water
½ cup packed light brown sugar
⅛ teaspoon salt
2 teaspoons whole cloves
2 cinnamon sticks, broken in pieces

Combine pineapple-pink grapefruit juice, cranberry juice, water, brown sugar, and salt in 4-quart saucepan. Tie cloves and cinnamon pieces in cheesecloth; add to saucepan. Heat to boiling; reduce heat and simmer 15 to 20 minutes. Discard spices; serve hot.

Jalapeno Cheese Balls

Makes 16 to 20 servings

1 pound shredded sharp Cheddar cheese
5 whole canned jalapeno peppers
1 large onion, quartered
3 cloves garlic
½ cup mayonnaise
1 cup chopped pecans
  Tortilla chips *or* crackers

Combine cheese, peppers, onion, and garlic in work bowl of food processor fitted with steel blade. Process with 2 or 3 on-off turns to blend. Add mayonnaise; process until smooth. Chill until firm; form into one large ball or 16 to 20 bite-sized balls. Chill until cheese is firm. Roll in pecans; chill again. Serve with tortilla chips.

Apple Nut Log

Makes one 6-inch log

1 8-ounce package cream cheese, softened
1 tablespoon apple juice
¼ teaspoon nutmeg
1 teaspoon fresh lemon juice
1 cup chopped apples
1 cup chopped pecans
  Wheat toast *or* wheat snack crackers

Combine cream cheese, apple juice, and nutmeg in mixing bowl; blend until smooth. Pour lemon juice over chopped apples. Add apples and ¾ cup of pecans to cheese mixture; blend well. Shape into one 6-inch log and roll in remaining chopped nuts. Wrap in plastic; refrigerate until ready to serve. Serve with wheat toast.

Caviar Pie

Makes one 9-inch pie

6 hard-boiled eggs, sieved
¼ cup unsalted butter at room temperature
2 8-ounce packages cream cheese, softened
  Chopped onion to taste
  Salt to taste
2 4-ounce jars caviar
  Sour cream

Combine eggs and butter in small bowl; mix well. Press into a 9-inch pie plate. Blend cheese with onion and salt. Turn into pie shell. Spread caviar over cheese mixture. Decorate with sour cream; use a pastry bag fitted with decorative tip, if desired. Serve with crackers.

Photo Opposite
MULLED PUNCH, ORIENTAL WALNUTS, CAVIAR PIE, MARINATED SHRIMP AND ARTICHOKE HEARTS, JALAPENO CHEESE BALLS, APPLE NUT LOG
Recipes from *Christmas and Holiday Cooking*, by Carol DeMasters, Ideals Publishing, 1985.

A Christmas Wish

There's a gentleness of friendship
In the Christmas cards that come;
There's a gladness in each message
As we read them, one by one.

We can see a Christmas setting
In the colors bright and gay.
We can feel a bond of friendship
Come our way on Christmas Day.

I'd like to see old friends today,
So Merry Christmas now I send
As down memory's lane I wander
And dream of you, dear friend.

Claire D. Sprague

Photo Opposite
SETTING UP THE CARDS
Monserrate J. Schwartz

Christmas Thoughts

Our feet may never climb the hills
In far Judea's strand,
Or walk the narrow winding streets
Within the Holy Land;
And yet, within our country here,
In city, farm, or town,
We can behold the Christmas star
Which brings the Savior down.
We can look out beyond the streets
Which hem our narrow way;
We can hear the angels' song
Within our sky today.
And in the eyes of someone near,
We may behold a dream—
To help a friend may be our role
Within the Christmas theme!

Alice Kennelly Roberts

Thinking of You

We will think of you at Christmas
When the fire is burning low,
And remember happy times we had
In the not so long ago.

We'll be there with you in spirit,
Christmas greetings to convey,
And we'll span the miles between us
Till another Christmas Day.

We will miss you all at Christmas
When the Yuletide bells chime,
And will hope we'll be together
At another Christmastime.

Esther Boomer Baker

Painting Overleaf
George Hinke

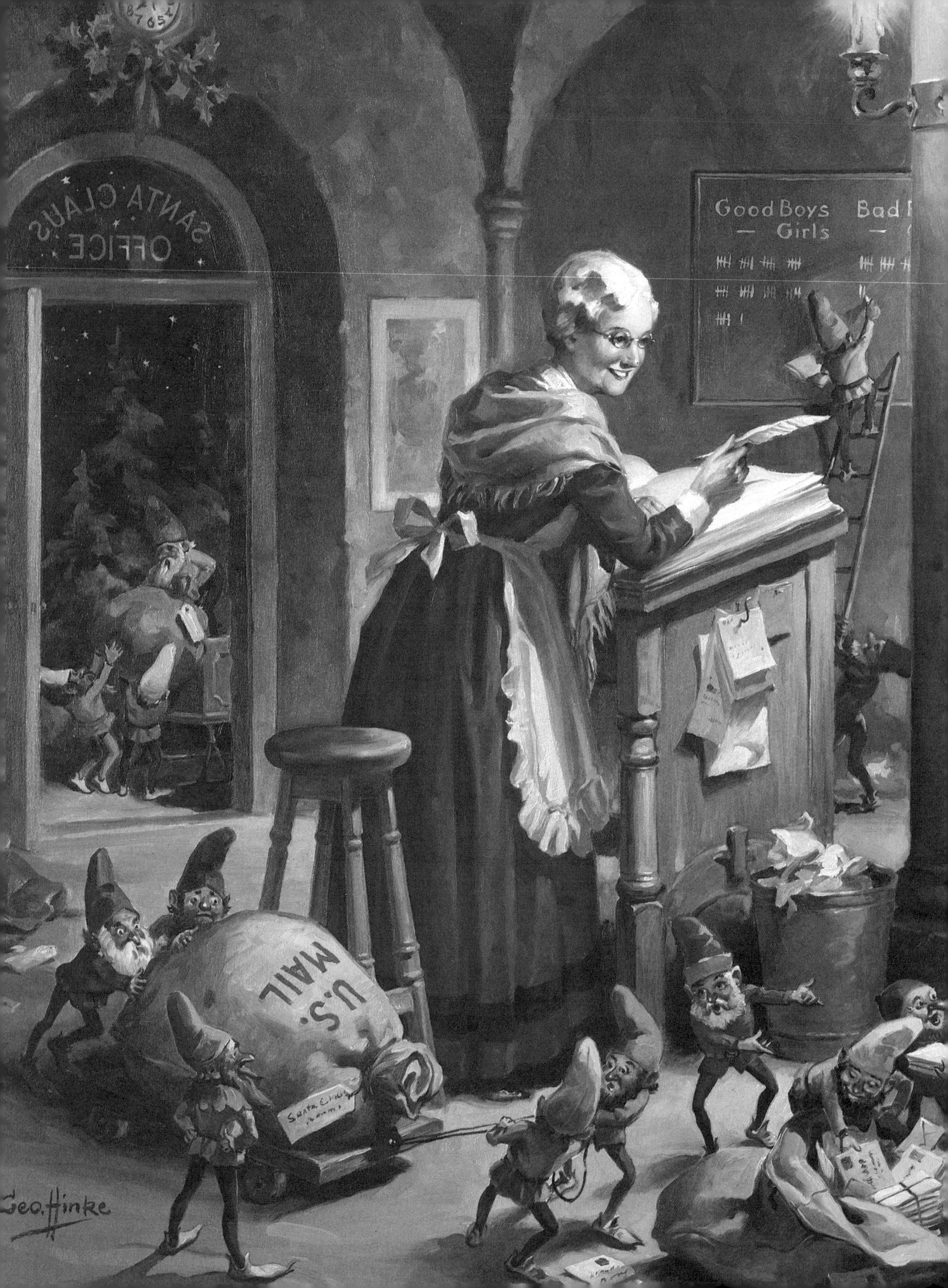
SANTA CLAUS
OFFICE
Good Boys
Girls
Bad
U.S. MAIL
Geo. Hinke

Country Chronicle

A Christmas snow falls softly on upland fields, piling star-shaped flakes of white on old stone walls, capping fence posts in hoods of lacy fluffiness. It transforms the boughs of evergreens into bowers under which the partridges seek shelter from the storm. A December snow always sparks memories of long gone Yuletides that link one generation to another. They tie the past to the present in a bow of love.

Memories may be of a child's awe admiring the brightly colored balls, bells, and tinsel which catch the gleam of lighted lamps. Memories may be the fragrance of a pine permeating every nook and cranny. They may be memories of Mother baking pies and cakes and cookies, of the aromas of spices and homemade bread, of bowls of crisp succulent apples, or of the tantalizing smell of freshly popped corn, buttered, warm, and ready to eat.

Customs change with the times, so do the memories. Each generation cherishes remembered Noels of childhood. Carolina, a niece whose home is in Vermont, wrote in her

Christmas letter of the family get-togethers at my parents' house. She remembers the excitement and expectancy, the bustling activity indoors while the wind tugged at the window blinds and strummed the needles of the pines. She recalls a December when she climbed upon her grandfather's knee and pleaded for a Christmas tree. Like Santa listening to the pleas of a child, my father listened to his granddaughter and went to the woods to bring in an evergreen. He also wrote her a poem, one which she cherishes and brings out each Christmas Eve to read to her own grandchildren as they sit on the floor by the lighted tree:

Today in snow that wet the knee,
I brought my grandchild's Christmas tree.
I climbed the hill where spruces grow;
The white world lay around below.
I found a tree that pleased the eye
And bore it homeward shoulder high.
I felt as light of foot as when
My eldest son was nine or ten.
Although the pines and I were there
With age's token in our hair,
I'll carry age, I'll have them know,
As lightly as they lift the snow.

Lansing Christman

Christmastime Is Here

Hearts are filled with laughter
And everybody's gay;
Passersby all greet you
In a warm and friendly way.

There's the greatest kind of feeling,
One that fills the heart with cheer
And lingers like a sweet refrain,
For Christmastime is here.

Lights are shining softly
Through windows sparkling bright;
Snow, like purest ermine,
Has dressed the world in white.

There's the greatest kind of feeling
Lingering round this time of year,
Making everybody happy
For Christmastime is here.

Carollers are singing
The Christmas carols sweet,
And the season's best of wishes
Are exchanged by all who meet.

Bells high in the steeple
Ring out in tones so clear,
Today was born a Savior
And Christmastime is here.

Mrs. Paul E. King

Christmas Eve

Light the candles one by one;
Share with us their flickering light.
Cares of men are put aside
On this star-illumined night.

Greens, as in the Middle Ages,
Decorate both walls and door;
Like scarlet drops on thorny leaves,
Holly berries shine once more.

In the past a kitchen custom,
Mistletoe, still waxen white,
Tells us, "Pick one pearly berry
For each kiss this festive night."

Strong young voices sing old carols
In unison or separate parts;
On a swelling tide of wonder,
Christmas magic fills our hearts.

Helen Ireland Hays

Reflections

See how the glowing candle casts
Its shadow on the wall!
Its scent of bayberry descends
With magic on us all.

It's Christmas Eve; the mantel boasts
Of stockings hung with care.
The buxom tree and ornaments
Bless the corner there.

Mom sits down to the organ and
Sweet carols softly plays;
It is a time to reminisce
'Bout long forgotten days.

The hour is late, the mantel clock
Strikes midnight, and we say:
"God bless you, each and everyone—
It's Merry Christmas Day!"

Georgia B. Adams

A Picture of a Village

There's a picture of a village
In a valley that I know,
Where the moon is shining brightly
On the newly fallen snow;
Where the air is crisp and frosty
And the night's clear as a bell;
And the evergreens are snow-tipped
On the hills and in the dell.

There's a picture of a village
In a valley that I love,
Where the snow-clad housetops glisten
Like the stars that shine above.
There's a beam that lights the pathway
From one doorstep to the next—
It's the special glow of friendliness
In the village I love best.

There's a picture of a village
In a valley dear to me,
And embellishing this picture
Is the frame of memory.

Loise Pinkerton Fritz

Photo Opposite
WESTFIELD, CT.
H. Armstrong Roberts

Christmas Reverie

As twilight hovers over Christmas
In the silent hush of day,
The busy cares and tension are
Laid aside to rest and play.

It's relaxing now to ponder
O'er our Christmas yesterdays;
With their happy joys and laughter,
Way back home our memory strays.

It seemed the holidays were different;
Different meanings, too, they had,
As we laid our plans for Christmas
With our sisters, Mom and Dad.

Popcorn balls and strings of popcorn,
Paper chains and garlands, too,
Little homemade bags of goodies
Trimmed the tree each year anew.

Today our tree is bright with color,
With its many shining lights;
Each year seeming to grow brighter
As we add some new delights.

Just as toys and children's playthings
Change from rag dolls to the new,
Would our children get the pleasure
From the toys that we once knew?

But, it's true, the order changes,
And we live new realms today;
But our hearts go back home on Christmas
To our own dear yesterday.

So, as twilight's shadows darken
O'er the day that Christ was born,
We have gladness for remembrance still,
In each new Christmas morn.

Edith M. Helstern

And it came to pass in those days, that there went out a decree from Caesar Augustus that all the world should be taxed.

(And this taxing was first made when Cyrenius was governor of Syria.)

And all went to be taxed, everyone to his own city.

And Joseph also went up from Galilee, out of the city of Nazareth, into Judea, unto the city of David, which is called Bethlehem, (because he was of the house and lineage of David:)

To be taxed with Mary, his espoused wife, being great with child.

And so it was, that while they were there, the days were accomplished that she should be delivered.

And she brought forth her firstborn son, and wrapped him in swaddling clothes, and laid him in a manger; because there was no room for them in the inn.

Luke 2:1-7

R. Adair

Mary's Prayer

But the angel said to her, "Do not be afraid, Mary, you have found favor with God. You will be with child and give birth to a son, and you are to give him the name Jesus. He will be great and will be called the Son of the Most High."

(Luke 1:30-32)

Tonight the skies are filled with
   stars, stars, stars!
O God! I have never seen beauty
   in such abundance!

And my heart has never beat
   with such a load of praise.
If only I had the talent
   of King David, then
     what a psalm I would
     sing for you this night!

But my thoughts tumble over themselves
   as I try to understand today's news—
   the news that I, a lowly maiden,
   have found favor with you—
with you, who formed dry land
      with a sweep of your hand,
    who hurled fire from heaven
      on the heads of Sodomites,
    who held back the Red Sea
      with the breath of your nostrils.

And yet, I know the truth
   of all the angel spoke.

Miracle of miracles—
   that I shall be mother
   of the Messiah!
But a twinge of sadness
   tugs at my heart
when I think of my
   own dear Joseph.

He will not understand
this wonder, Lord.

He is too used to dealing with reality:
   the smell of shavings and sawdust,
   the rhythm of tireless planing,
   the strength of his own strong arms
     reshaping the cedars from Lebanon.

Angels and visions and impossibilities
   are foreign stuff
     to my carpenter.

And how shall I make him understand
   that I am virgin still—

but with child!

O loving Lord,
   do me this one favor:

let my beloved Joseph
     believe—

let this miracle
   be as real to him
     as oxen yokes and
     ax handles.

Let him know that
   it is your hand—
that you, O Lord, have done it.

Almighty God,
   add to this miraculous news

     just one miracle more—

let Joseph believe!

Mary Lou Carney

Because Joseph her husband was a righteous man and did not want to expose her to public disgrace, he had in mind to divorce her quietly. But after he had considered this, an angel of the Lord appeared to him in a dream and said, "Joseph son of David, do not be afraid to take Mary home as your wife, because what is conceived in her is from the Holy Spirit. She will give birth to a son, and you are to give him the name Jesus, because he will save his people from their sins." When Joseph woke up, he did what the angel of the Lord had commanded him and took Mary home as his wife.

(Matthew 1:19-21, 24)

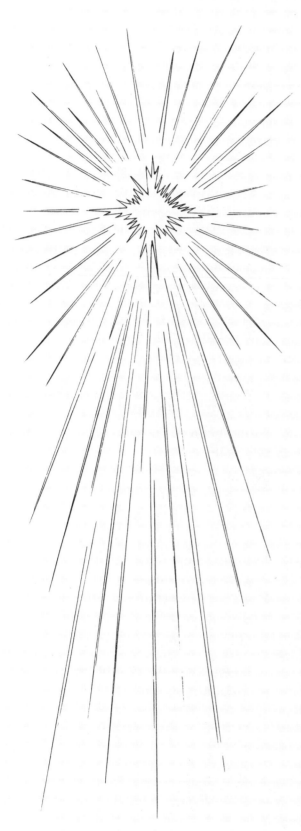

Behold the Child

Behold the child in the manger bed—
His grip is strong,
His cheeks so red.

Behold the star in the sky tonight—
It just appeared
And shines so bright.

Behold the host of angels there—
Oh, hear their song;
It fills the air!

Shepherds come, and strangers too!
Who is the child
They come to woo?

Behold the gifts these wise men bring!
A child so poor. . .
Is he a king?

O holy night! O Bethlehem!
Behold the child—
Come worship him!

Clay Harrison

John Walter

Nativity Journey

Mary closed her eyes wearily and sighed, finding it difficult to breathe deeply with the weight of her unborn child pressing upon her. The hot sun scorched her skin, and the gritty desert dust sifted into the folds of her robe. How many hours, she wondered, how many days had they traveled? It had seemed an adventure at first, setting off for the city of David with Joseph. It would be a welcome break from the stares and gossip of Nazareth's narrow streets. But now she wondered. Her mother's glare of disapproval as they left home was still vivid in Mary's mind.

"It's not wise," her mother had warned, "the baby's birth is too near." Mary was not willing to leave Joseph's side, even if it meant having her child far from her mother's capable hands.

She sighed again and opened her burning eyes. The landscape shimmered in the heat and the little donkey stumbled on a loose rock. Mary's bulk caused her to lose her balance easily, and when the animal mis-stepped, she slid awkwardly off, landing unceremoniously on the ground.

Joseph was beside her immediately. "Are you all right? Are you injured?" His deep brown eyes were filled with concern and worry.

"Only my pride is damaged, dear Joseph," she replied with a rueful smile. "Come, sit beside me for a moment and let's rest a bit."

The two weary travelers shared a date cake and a drink of water.

"Will it be much longer?" Mary asked, her eyes searching the horizon for a sign of their destination.

Joseph turned to look at her. Streaks of dusty sweat marked her cheeks, and wisps of dark hair clung to her damp forehead. Gently, he stroked her face with his calloused hand. "You have been so strong, my little one," he said softly, and she rewarded his kind words with a tired smile. "It won't be much longer now. I think tonight we may reach Bethlehem. It should be just over that far rise there. Then you may rest in a clean soft bed again and eat a warm meal."

Joseph helped her up and Mary felt a sharp twinge in her lower back. She gasped and Joseph looked alarmed.

"It's nothing, nothing—just a kink from sitting on the ground. I think I'll walk a bit and give poor Ephram a rest." She patted the tired little donkey and he whinnied his appreciation. Then she and Joseph resumed their trek.

The white sun finally started its descent across the western sky, and a breeze came up, refreshing the weary couple.

"Look," Joseph said, pointing across the rocky landscape, "other pilgrims."

Mary watched the tiny figures in the distance and wondered if they had traveled as far as she. The twinges in her back were more frequent now, and she found it difficult to keep pace with Joseph. "I think I'd like to ride a while," she called, and Joseph lifted her onto Ephram's dusty back.

She watched Joseph as he led them over the uneven ground. His shoulders were broad and his legs strong and muscular. What a good father he will be, she thought and smiled at the picture of Joseph frolicking around the small carpenter's shop with a little one riding on his shoulders and clinging to the thick dark hair already showing just a hint of silver. Suddenly, tears filled her eyes as the picture faded and the weight of the responsibility fell upon her. How can we train any child, especially this very special child? she wondered. Uncertainty and apprehension crowded her thoughts, and she began to weep softly.

"Look!" Joseph's shout startled her and she quickly dried her eyes with the corner of her shawl. She followed his direction and saw the irregular skyline of Bethlehem to the south.

More and more pilgrims joined them on the dusty trails leading into town. Everyone seemed rushed to get to the city before nightfall. Even Joseph picked up the pace and poor Ephram protested with a wheezing bray. The sky was quickly darkening and already Mary could see the early stars. Their brightness seemed exaggerated in the cooling air, and one stood brilliantly over the city itself. Its beauty captured Mary's attention and she called to Joseph, "See the star, Joseph! It is as if God lights our way!"

Joseph turned and grinned at her. "Your relief at reaching Bethlehem has turned you into a poet, Mary!" he teased. "I would be pleased if God saw fit to find us a pleasant place to spend the night."

As they entered the city, they were jostled by the hurrying throngs. Mary's pain was increasing steadily, yet she hesitated to alarm Joseph. He was already concerned.

Joseph stopped several travelers to inquire about directions to an inn. Their comments weren't encouraging. Mary overheard the words, "full, crowded, no room'' and her shoulders drooped. Still, Joseph continued, stopping, inquiring, knocking on door after door.

Mary's pains became more intense and she groaned softly.

"Mary, what is it? Has the time come?" Joseph lifted her off Ephram and she began to cry.

"Oh, Joseph, I'm so tired. Just find me a place, any place, where I can lie down and be out of the crowds and the dust. Please, Joseph." She buried her face in his cloak and clenched her jaw as the next pain came.

Gently, he carried her, marveling at how light she was even in her pregnancy. They stopped at three more places and were leaving the third, when the wife of the innkeeper ran after them and pulled on Joseph's sleeve.

"Is your wife with child?" she asked, concern

clouding her plump features.

"Yes and about to deliver, I fear," Joseph replied.

"Come," the woman insisted and led them around the side of the inn to a small cave-like enclosure where the animals were stabled for the night. "It isn't much," she said softly, regret filling her voice, "but it will be clean and quiet." Efficiently, she set about heaping clean straw in a vacant corner, then she removed her shawl and arranged it over the soft, sweet bed. "Put her here and tie the donkey outside," she ordered, at ease in charge of things. "Now you run along and fetch some clean cloths from inside. Ask my daughter, Myra, she will know where to look for them. Leave us now, this is woman's work."

Mary grimaced with pain and the older woman smoothed the hair from her forehead. "There, there now, little one. You will do fine and soon you will have a bouncing baby to hold in your arms."

Her manner was reassuring and Mary felt more calm. "He will be a boy," she whispered softly, "and he will be God's son."

The innkeeper's wife smiled indulgently and patted Mary's cheek. "Yes, well, they are all God's children, aren't they, dear?"

Mary turned her face away and a tear slipped down her cheek. Will it always be this way? she wondered as she caught sight of the brilliant star above the inn. Will they never understand?

For hours she labored there while the cows and sheep and little Ephram gazed on in profound silence. Had they shared in this miracle of birth? Mary wondered. She suddenly felt part of earth and sky and nature itself—struggling to bring forth offspring; to see new life burst forth from old.

When the child came at last, the woman wrapped him in the cloths Joseph had brought and laid him at his mother's breast. Exhausted and exultant, Mary studied the tiny face, the pursing lips, the age-old newborn eyes, and the babe sighed and nuzzled close. She traced the flawless cheek with her finger and pondered as she held her slumbering son. Her mind could not grasp it all, but her mother's heart, awakened by the Spirit of the Living God, began to comprehend this culminating work of love. She gazed upon her child and saw her Father's will. For him, she knew, the journey was just beginning.

Pamela Kennedy

And there were in the same country shepherds abiding in the field, keeping watch over their flock by night.

And, lo, an angel of the Lord came upon them, and the glory of the Lord shone round about them: and they were sore afraid.

And the angel said unto them, "Fear not: for, behold, I bring you good tidings of great joy, which will be to all people.

"For unto you is born this day in the city of David a Savior, which is Christ the Lord.

"And this shall be a sign unto you; Ye shall find the babe wrapped in swaddling cloths, lying in a manger."

And suddenly there was with the angel a multitude of the heavenly host praising God, and saying,

"Glory to God in the highest,
And on earth peace,
good will toward men."

And it came to pass, as the angels were gone away from them into heaven, the shepherds said one to another, "Let us now go even unto Bethlehem, and see this thing which is come to pass, which the Lord hath made known unto us."

And they came with haste, and found Mary and Joseph, and the babe lying in a manger.

Luke 2:8-16

Photo Opposite
BEHOLD, AN ANGEL
The Photo Source

GLORIA

A Peaceful Christmas be thine.

The Meaning of Christmas

Last night I started thinking
What Christmas means to me,
And in my deep pondering
I found these things to be.

It wasn't the excitement,
The rushing to and fro,
Nor was it all the buying
That made my spirit glow.

It wasn't all the tinsel,
Nor lighted Christmas trees—
Carols, music, ringing bells—
That brought me ecstasies.

It wasn't burning candles
Nor wreaths and mistletoe,
And sealed up pretty bundles,
All tied with fancy bows.

It wasn't stockings hanging
From off the mantlepiece,
Nor happy children laughing
That brought me inner peace.

But just the thought of Christmas,
A manger drab and poor,
With little baby Jesus
Holds much for me in store.

A star shone from the heavens
That cold and wintry night,
Where wise men and poor shepherds
Walked on beneath its light.

Yes, Christmas has a meaning
To me and others, too,
Beyond the joy of giving,
A meaning deep and true.

Gertrude Rudberg

Christmastime

Christmas bells are ringing out
Across the land today;
They ring on streets, in belfries high,
And on the horse-drawn sleigh.

Christmas lights are shining bright
In windows, streets, and trees,
Making rainbows in the snow
And shadows of the leaves.

Christmas carols fill the air;
There's singing in each heart.
Christ alone has caused the music,
Made the Christmas carols start.

Herald out then, all ye people,
Blow the trumpets, sing with mirth;
For today was born a Savior—
Christ the Lord, of royal birth.

Mrs. Paul E. King

Photo Opposite
CHRISTMAS MORNING
Fred Dole

Angels of Christmas

Outside the church on the snow-lined sidewalk which had been shoveled hours before, the celestial sisters hurried along: organdy angels crushed beneath wool plaid coats, cheesecloth wings folded under their arms. Their earthly mothers with earthly brothers in tow carried brown grocery bags containing the shepherds' bathrobes and cane staffs. In trios and quartets on the curb, fathers talked quietly, nervously waiting for the service to begin.

Tonight was the night of the annual Christmas program, a scene that was repeated at some time or another in each church in the community.

The program had been practiced for weeks. At choir rehearsal after school, the voices had sung again the verses that did not need to be recommitted to memory. During Sunday morning church school, the shepherds and angels had entered and exited the choir loft stage, rehearsing the ageless words they had been assigned, while the baby doll Jesus and Mary and Joseph (that sanctified couple who never had a line) formed the classic tableau.

Although I often sang in the children's choir or occasionally accompanied them on the piano, I remember that one year I was one of the angels, tinsel halo bobby pinned to my hair. The stepladder hilltop, draped with a white bed sheet, seemed a precarious perch for us Bethlehem angels and probably accounts for the unheavenly scowl on our faces in the Christmas snapshot.

Certainly Christmastime is the loveliest time to enter a church: the month of candlelight, red poinsettias, and the overpowering scent of pine. At the front of the sanctuary, we always had a real Christmas tree, the tallest one, surely, in my December world, bedecked with a miscellany of family ornaments and lights.

The congregation sat for this Sunday evening program in the same places they occupied for the Sunday morning service. Families in their family pews visited a little more boisterously than they did on Sunday mornings since the occasion was one of seasonal joy that is both sacred and secular.

There was an hour of special music (always a vocal solo of "I Wonder as I Wander" by the minister's son); eager recitations of St. Luke from red-dressed children whose parents nervously laughed and then spontaneously applauded; a few words of meditation from the uncommonly relaxed pastor; and then the song leader stood beside the piano and led the audience in the carols for which no hymnals were needed. We always closed with "Silent Night."

At that point, Santa Claus burst through the door of the pastor's study and into the sanctuary. It was not in the least anticlimactic, despite the regularity of his annual visit.

The small children could not be restrained and rushed out to meet him. The adults smiled and at last forgot their own children. The older youngsters whispered knowingly of Santa's identity, naming an absent deacon.

Santa laughed and joked and with the assistance of the ushers, handed out to the children from each family a small brown sack heavy with peppermints, candy ribbons, chocolates, candied orange slices, and Brazil nuts.

Breaking up the evening was difficult to do. Once on, the gossamer wings seemed delightfully comfortable after all; it was hard letting go of what we had. Reluctantly, the congregation moved into the night from the church whose heavy leaded window had lighted from within, rather than from without.

The winter air did not seem so cold.

Cindy Hoffman

Yuletide Halo

A Christmas tree cut in the woods,
Brought over drifting snow
With laughter, shouts, and merry songs,
And pink cheek's ruddy glow.

Green sprigs of holly, mistletoe
Trim every door and wall;
Bright leaves and sprays of bittersweet
Saved lovingly from fall.

A tang of oranges tucked away,
Of cinnamon and spice,
Drift out to vie with baking pie
So Christmasy and nice.

The fireplace shows a golden glow,
A halo, I believe,
Encircles earth and home and Heaven
On blessed Christmas Eve.

Dan A. Hoover

Photo Opposite
CHRISTMAS LAMP
Fred Sieb

The Christmas Assembly

Today is the Christmas assembly.

I sit with other parents
    on brown metal chairs,
all watching the orchestra
        file into the gym,
        wondering when our children
        became so tall,
            so grown-up,
            so serious.

Florescent lights glint off
    brightly polished baritones,
    highly buffed cellos.

Stuffy air is shattered by
    scrambled sounds of squeals and
        plinks,
    rumbling groans of bows
        drawn across taut strings
as each musician
    tackles the task of tuning.

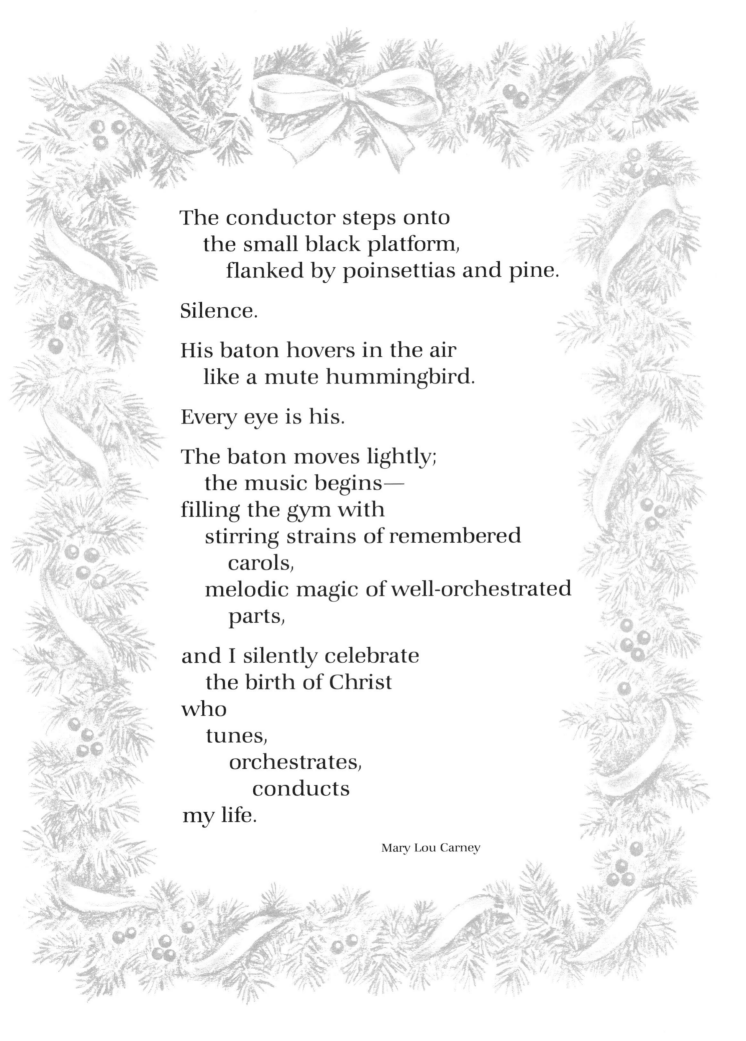

The conductor steps onto
   the small black platform,
      flanked by poinsettias and pine.

Silence.

His baton hovers in the air
   like a mute hummingbird.

Every eye is his.

The baton moves lightly;
   the music begins—
filling the gym with
   stirring strains of remembered
      carols,
   melodic magic of well-orchestrated
      parts,

and I silently celebrate
   the birth of Christ
who
   tunes,
      orchestrates,
         conducts
my life.

Mary Lou Carney

Perfect Gift

I do not ask for lavish gifts
Nor satin gowns to wear.
I have no need for jeweled combs
Or flowers in my hair.
I only ask on Christmas Day
To find when I arise,
That I may see the world again
With a child's unclouded eyes.

Phyllis M. Flaig

When You Were Only Two

So small a child—just two—
She stands, in ecstasy,
Before the wondrous sight
Of lighted Christmas tree.

No brighter than her eyes,
The lights above her hair;
Please hold her, Lord, I pray,
A moment longer there,

Before the wings of time
Rush on in hurried flight
To end a moment's joy
On this Christmas night.

So small she is, 'tis true,
Yet somehow grows so fast,
And these precious moments
Are gone—they do not last.

Hold her a moment more,
With life so eager—new—
She is so like you, Lord,
When you were only two.

Alice B. Johnson

Photo Opposite
THE WONDER OF CHRISTMAS
H. Armstrong Roberts

Annie and Willie's Prayer

This favorite from many years ago is presented in response to numerous requests from our reader friends.

'Twas the eve before Christmas; goodnight had been said,
And Annie and Willie had crept into bed.
There were tears on their pillows and tears in their eyes,
And each little bosom was heaving with sighs.

For tonight their stern father's command had been given
That they should retire precisely at seven
Instead of at eight; for they troubled him more
With questions unheard of than ever before.

He told them he thought this delusion a sin—
No such thing as Santa Claus ever had been.
And he hoped after this, he would never more hear
How he scrambled down chimneys with presents each year.

And this was the reason that two little heads
So restlessly tossed on their soft downy beds.
Eight, nine, and the clock in the steeple tolled ten;
Not a word had been spoken by either till then.

When Willie's sad face from the blanket did peep,
And whispered, "Dear Annie, is you fast asleep?"
"Why, no, brother Willie," a sweet voice replied,
"I've tried in vain, but I can't shut my eyes.

"For somehow, it makes me so sorry because
Dear Papa said there is no Santa Claus.
Now we know that there is, and it can't be denied,
For he came every year before Mamma died.

"But then I am thinking that she used to pray,
And God would hear everything Mamma would say.
And perhaps she asked him to send Santa Claus here,
With sacks full of presents he brought every year."

"Well, why tan't we pray dest as Mamma did then,
And ask him to send him with presents aden?"
"I've been thinking so, too," and without a word more,
Four little bare feet bounded out on the floor.

Four little knees the soft carpet pressed,
And two tiny hands were clasped close to each breast.
"Now, Willie, you know we must firmly believe
That the presents we ask for we're sure to receive.

"You must wait just as still, till I say the 'amen,'
And by that you will know that your turn has come then.
Dear Jesus, look down on my brother and me,
And grant us the favor we are asking of thee:

"I want a wax dolly, a tea set and ring,
And an ebony work box that shuts with a spring.
Bless Papa, dear Jesus, and cause him to see
That Santa Claus loves us far better than he.

"Don't let him get fretful and angry again
At dear brother Willie, and Annie.
   Amen."
"Pease, Desus, 'et Santa Taus tum down tonight,
And bring us some presents before it is light.

"I want he should div me a nice 'ittle sed,
With b'ite shiny runners, and all painted red;
A box full of tandy, a book and a toy,
Then Desus, I'll be a dood boy.
   Amen."

Their prayers being ended, they raised up their heads,
And with hearts light and cheerful again sought their beds.
They were soon lost in slumber, both peaceful and deep,
And with fairies in dreamland were roaming in sleep.

Eight, nine, and the little French clock had struck ten,
Ere the father had thought of his children again.
He seems now to hear Annie's suppressed sighs,
And to see the big tears stand in Willie's blue eyes.

"I was harsh with my darlings," he mentally said,
"And should not have sent them so early to bed;
But then, I was troubled—my feelings found vent,
For bank stock today has gone down ten percent.

"But of course they've forgotten their troubles ere this,
And that I denied them the thrice-asked-for kiss.
But just to make sure I'll steal up to their door,
For I never spoke harsh to my darlings before."

So saying, he softly ascended the stairs,
And arrived at the door to hear both of their prayers.
His Annie's "bless Papa" draws forth the big tears,
And Willie's grave promise falls sweet on his ears.

"Strange, strange, I'd forgotten," said he with a sigh,
"How I longed when a child to have Christmas draw
  nigh.
I'll atone for my harshness," he inwardly said,
"By answering their prayers, ere I sleep in my bed."

Then he turned to the stairs, and softly went down,
Threw off velvet slippers and silk dressing-gown,
Donned hat, coat, and boots, and was out in the street,
A millionaire facing the cold driving sleet.

Nor stopped he until he had bought everything,
From a box full of candy to a tiny gold ring.
Indeed, he kept adding so much to his store,
That the various presents outnumbered a score.

Then homeward he turned with his holiday load,
And with Aunt Mary's aid in the nursery 'twas stowed.
Miss dolly was seated beneath a pine tree,
By the side of a table spread out for a tea.

A work box well filled in the center was laid,
And on it the ring for which Annie had prayed.
A soldier in uniform stood by a sled,
With bright shining runners, and all painted red.

There were balls, dogs, and horses, books pleasing to
  see,
And birds of all colors were perched in the tree,
While Santa Claus, laughing, stood up in the top,
As if getting ready more presents to drop.

And as the fond father the picture surveyed,
He thought for his trouble he had amply been paid.
And said to himself, as he brushed off a tear,
"I'm happier tonight than I've been for a year.

"I've enjoyed more true pleasure than ever before,
What care I if bank stock falls ten percent more.
Hereafter I'll make it a rule, I believe,
To have Santa Claus visit us each Christmas Eve."

So thinking, he gently extinguished the light,
Then tripped down the stairs to retire for the night.
As soon as the beams of the bright morning sun
Put the darkness to flight, and the stars, one by one,

Four little blue eyes out of sleep open'd wide,
And at the same moment the presents espied.
Then out of their beds they sprang with a bound,
And the very gifts prayed for were all of them found.

They laughed and they cried in their innocent glee,
And shouted for Papa to come quick and see
What presents old Santa Claus brought in the night,
(Just the things that they wanted) and left before light.

"And now," added Annie, in a voice soft and low,
"You'll believe there's a Santa Claus, Papa, I know."
While dear little Willie climbed up on his knee,
Determined no secret between them should be,

And told in soft whispers how Annie had said
That their dear blessed Mamma, so long ago dead,
Used to kneel down and pray by the side of her chair,
And that God up in Heaven had answered her prayer!

"Then we dot up and prayed dust as well as we tould,
And Dod answered our prayers; now wasn't he dood?"
"I should say that he was if he sent you all these,
And knew just what presents my children would
  please.

("Well, well, let him think so, the dear little elf;
'Twould be cruel to tell him I did it myself.")
Blind father! who caused your proud heart to relent;
And the hasty word spoken so soon to repent?

'Twas Lord Jesus who bade you steal softly upstairs,
And made you his agent to answer their prayers.

Sophia P. Snow

Christmas Joy

Tuck some joy into each toy
That you have Santa send.
Ask God to bless each greeting card
You mail out to a friend.

Shout Yuletide cheer into each ear
As you greet passersby.
Let your voice ring in a carol
That echoes to the sky.

Be oh, so bold with silver and gold
As you trim your Christmas tree.
Put a shiny star way up high
For everyone to see.

Have your feast but look to the east
For the Star of Bethlehem.
Wear a joyous smile and pause awhile
To remember Jerusalem.

Remember Christ's birth upon the earth
On this joyous Christmas Day.
Thank God above for a Savior to love
When you kneel down to pray.

Florence Weber

JOHN DRUCKENMILLER

Photo Opposite
THE TOYS OF CHRISTMAS
Fred Sieb

Santa Claus

Now this is the thing I'd like to know:
How Santa Claus can step in snow
With a world of toys upon his back
And leave not the slightest hint of a track;
How one so big and round and fat
Can slip through a hole that would choke a rat
And smoke so thick it can hide the trees,
And never even cough, nor sneeze!

Well, my child, it does seem queer,
But it's just like this: you're standing here
Thinking of things you cannot see
And wondering how such things can be.
The fact is, child, nobody knows
What Santa looks like nor where he goes,
For Santa Claus is a sprite that lives
In the heart that loves, in the heart that gives.
He may be here and he may be there,
You are likely to find him anywhere.
But really, folk are so very blind
They can't see the spirit that gives and loves,
So we picture a thing in coat and gloves
Like a jolly old man who is round and fat.
And we love the thing, and we look at that;
And being a spirit, through and through,
Of course, he can do what a spirit can do.

But the Santa himself we never see,
The Santa in you, the Santa in me.

Leigh Hanes

A Christmas Invitation

It was nearly time to close the shop
One snowy Christmas Eve,
When a ragged little fellow clutched
The owner by his sleeve.

"Mister, sir," the urchin cried,
"I know it's time to leave,
But you have just one dolly left
And it is Christmas Eve.
Don't you think she'll be unhappy, sir,
Alone on Christmas Day
Without the other dollies here
With whom she used to play?
I could invite her to my house
To spend the day with sister;
I'm sure she'd take good care of her,
Could I do that, please mister?"

The owner turned to look into
The earnest little face,
Remembering a Christmas Day
In another time and place,
When his own little sister
Had waited hopefully
For just one tiny little doll
Beneath her Christmas tree.

Then tenderly he took the doll
And gave her to the lad,
"Your Christmas invitation, son,
Will make her very glad."

Dorris Gainder

How God Made Kittens

I think I know how God made you,
With your little elfin face.
He took a tiny pansy
That bloomed with extra grace,
And added twelve white whiskers
And shiny topaz eyes,
An extra touch of velvet
For some small child's surprise.
He took some little stickers
From a wee, wild baby rose,
And made some teeny mittens
And a tiny, wet, pink nose,

A bit of love and beauty,
Some playful, soft allure,
And hid inside you a purr-box
Filled to the brim with purr.
A little bell of silver
He gave for your meow.
"I'll give the world a kitten
To go with its Bow-wow."
He said, "I've made a doggie,
Kids need a kitten, too!"
And so God gave to children
The precious gift of you!

Louise Weibert Sutton

Photo Opposite
CHRISTMAS KITTEN
Barry L. Runk
Grant Heilman Photography

For Santa's Sake

He was almost six that winter—
So grown up, and yet so young.
"Mommie," said my little angel,
As the towels he neatly hung,

"Please help me write a letter,
When the dishes are all done.
One to Santa Claus to tell him
I'd like a holster and a gun."

I dried my hands and held him close,
This little boy so dear.
"Don't you remember, darling,
What we talked about last year?"

He nodded as my lips he touched
With a chubby little hand,
Then came the words I can't forget,
Nor fully understand.

"I know there is no Santa Claus,
And so does brother Jim,
But I must write to him so he'll *think*
We still believe in him."

Lois M. Reed

Christmas with Little Women

Louisa May Alcott

"Christmas won't be Christmas without any presents," grumbled Jo, lying on the rug.

"It's so dreadful to be poor!" sighed Meg, looking down at her old dress.

"We've got Father and Mother and each other," said Beth contentedly from her corner.

The four young faces on which the firelight shone brightened at the cheerful words.

"The reason Mother proposed not having any presents this Christmas was because it is going to be a hard winter for everyone," Meg said. "She thinks we ought not to spend money for pleasure."

Meg, the oldest of the four, was sixteen, and very pretty. Fifteen-year-old Jo was very tall and thin with a comical nose and sharp gray eyes. Elizabeth—or Beth—was a rosy, bright-eyed girl of thirteen. Amy, though the youngest, was a regular snow maiden, with blue eyes and yellow hair.

"Glad to find you so merry, my girls," said a cheery voice at the door, and the girls turned to welcome a tall, motherly lady. She was not elegantly dressed, but the girls thought the gray cloak and unfashionable bonnet covered the most splendid mother in the world. The girls flew about, trying to make things comfortable, each in her own way.

Jo was the first to wake in the gray dawn of Christmas morning. She woke Meg with a "Merry Christmas."

"Where is Mother?" asked Meg, as she and Jo ran down half an hour later.

"Goodness only knows. Some poor creeter come a-beggin', and your ma went straight off to see what was needed," replied Hannah, who had lived with the family since Meg was born.

"She will be back soon, I think," said Meg.

"There's Mother," cried Jo, as a door slammed and footsteps sounded in the hall.

"Merry Christmas, Marmee! Many of them!" they cried, in chorus.

"Merry Christmas, little daughters! But I want to say one word before we sit down. Not far away from here lies a poor woman with a newborn baby. Six children are huddled into one bed to

from *Christmas with Little Women*
by Louisa May Alcott, illustrated by Russ Flint,
copyright © 1986 by Ideals Publishing, Nashville, Tennessee.

keep from freezing, for they have no fire. There is nothing to eat over there, and the oldest boy came to tell me they were suffering hunger and cold. My girls, will you give them your breakfast as a Christmas present?"

They were all unusually hungry, and for a minute no one spoke—only a minute, for Jo exclaimed impetuously, "I'm so glad you came before we began!"

"May I go and help carry the things to the poor little children?" asked Beth eagerly.

"I shall take the cream and the muffins," added Amy, giving up the articles she most liked.

Meg was already covering the buckwheats, and piling the bread onto one big plate.

"I thought you'd do it," said Mrs. March, smiling as if satisfied.

A poor, bare, miserable room it was, with broken windows, no fire, ragged bedclothes, a sick mother, wailing baby, and a group of pale, hungry children cuddled under one old quilt. How the big eyes stared and the blue lips smiled as the girls went in! "It is good angels come to us!" said the poor woman, crying for joy.

"Funny angels in hoods and mittens," said Jo, and set them laughing.

In a few minutes it really did seem as if kind spirits had been at work there. Hannah, who had carried wood, made a fire, and stopped up the broken panes with old hats and her own cloak. Mrs. March gave the mother tea and gruel, and comforted her with promises of help, while she dressed the little baby. The girls spread the table, set the children round the fire, and fed them like so many hungry birds—laughing and talking.

That was a very happy breakfast, though they didn't get any of it. When they went away, leaving comfort behind, I think there were not in all the city four merrier people than the hungry little girls who gave away their breakfasts on Christmas morning.

My Most Cherished Christmas Gift

It began with a small strip of cloth, approximately two by eight inches, on which someone had stitched lines of bright thread in hither and thither design. The stitches were all equal in size and tension—the product of a well-operating sewing machine.

It was 1953, a time of magic, for love turns everything to magic and we were in love. It was also my first time to share Christmas with the family of the man who was to become my husband the following Valentine's Day.

When I opened the small box (I expected it to contain a bracelet or necklace), I stared at it in amazement and a bit of disappointment, wondering about that tiny bit of cloth.

"There's more!" he told me, the now-familiar gleam in his chocolate brown eyes. "In the basement!"

"The basement?" More amazement.

So we all trooped down to the old basement beneath the warm brick house and there, standing shiny bright on clean newspapers, was a sewing machine.

It was not a new sewing machine. New sewing machines were things dreams were made of, and much too expensive for new brides. It was a sewing machine, nevertheless, stripped of its old scratches and varnish and treadle. It gleamed in oaken splendor as a result of loving labor in sanding and polishing. The old machine was even revitalized with a new electric motor, straight from the pages of a mail order catalog.

We came from families where it was taken for granted that you canned and preserved most of the food which went on the family table, just as you cut and sewed almost every item of clothing which went on the family's individual backs. His gift to me was a way of sustaining a tradition, and our first piece of furniture.

With it I sewed the curtains and cushions which first graced our humble four rooms. I stitched away many a long night as he slept in the next room, exhausted from his long day in the fields. There were dresses for me to wear to the office and new sports shirts for him. And soon, I was planning tiny things, piecing them together on that sturdy old machine, adding teddy bears and flowers with hand embroidery. Twice the small gowns and sacques and blankets were tucked away in a bottom drawer with the pastel shades of pink and blue dampened by tears of broken dreams. All that changed one bright February morn, and the sun shone so brightly at our home we hardly needed to turn on the lights. Our daughter was born and two years later, a son helped brighten our home. To our surprise (somewhat), five years later another beautiful daughter was born.

That old sewing machine kept me busy. We spent many intimate hours together; stitching ruffled dresses in progressive sizes, struggling with the corded seams of pint-sized cowboy shirts, fitting pattern pieces very carefully onto remnants, and turning all the leftover scraps into minute doll dresses and shirts for teddy bears.

Later, there were Halloween costumes: a comic book hero, a witch, a leopard, a toreador, and even a perky black and white skunk with a (thanks to Daddy) wired tail which made it every bit as handsome as any of Disney's creations!

Like my mother before me, I became a 4-H leader, and little girls from fancier homes than ours learned to sew on that kindly old machine. It insisted on straight seams, though, and did cause a few tears. Later, those same little girls entrusted me with making their prom dresses and wedding gowns, knowing the seams would be as straight as only that old machine could do.

Paper patterns grew tattered and torn as we used them over and over with variations and adjustments. The spool box became cluttered with tangles of every conceivable color. Buttons found their separate ways into a tin fruitcake box which rattled delightfully when shaken. Its contents were used not only to march proudly down the front or back of a sewing project, but also as farm produce carried to market in small metal trucks and as delectable morsels served up on tin tea sets. Rows of buttons on the rug were carefully counted, one, two, three . . . and colors were learned, blue, yellow, green, red.

Pants knees were patched and patched again. Hems were let down and trim stitched over the white lines to cover the fade marks. Collars on work shirts were turned (oh, how we hated that chore). And pockets, which had been made untrustworthy by more important things than coins (such as nuts, bolts, and colored pebbles), were reinforced.

Yes, we spent many hours together, that sewing machine and I. As the needle plunged up and down, thread paying out from the wooden spool, I planned menus and surprises and wrote invisible poems in my mind. I worried over finances and stewed over the United Nations veto powers and my choices in the next election. Some hours were delightful and fun-filled, and some were just plain work.

But that old machine never let me down. All it asked was an occasional squirt of oil and once in a while, a new light bulb or belt. Seldom does a woman find as true a friend. That old machine was there when we became one. It helped turn a house into a home and it dressed our babes far beyond what our meager financial means would have permitted if we had purchased "ready-mades."

Years later, I received another sewing machine—the very best, top of the line model. Its cabinet had never been kicked or scratched, and it purred every stitch in quiet splendor.

By now, however, we could afford to buy draperies and slipcovers, and teenagers don't always appreciate Mother's choice of pattern and fabric. The promised magic wasn't to be found in those fancy zigzag stitches; not for those who had known and lived by the purity of the straightforward. That beautiful, fancy new machine, though no longer new, still has very low mileage.

My old sewing machine wasn't fancy, but it was special. It wasn't just a Christmas gift of which dreams were made. It did much, much more. It *made* dreams come true!

Dorthy M. Ross

My Favorite Time

The week after Christmas
I like best of all;
The rushing is over
And friends come to call.

The fruitcake is ready,
The cookies are made,
And leisure for reading
The cards on parade.

There's time for relaxing,
Old dreams to recall,
The week after Christmas
I like best of all.

Hilda Butler Farr

Winter Magic

The picture I see on my windowpane
Is one of a landscape—clear and plain.
It was painted there in the night's still hush,
By winter's hand, with an icy brush.

This work of art now being shown
Is really not my very own,
But lent to me for just a day—
I cannot hope for it to stay.

And strange is the fact, if you could but know,
The scene is not of winter and snow;
But of fern and palm branches, in relief,
And tropical trees on a sandy reef.

Could it be that old winter, so deft and quick,
Is showing me a sleight of hand trick
To make me think it is getting warm—
To coax me out in an icy storm?

I'll just sit and wait by my fireside here
Till my windowpane is smooth and clear;
Then seeing all things in reality,
I'll know if the outside beckons me.

Vera E. Maddry

The Earth's Hibernation

The days shorten,
winter grows near,
the temperature drops,
and snowflakes appear.
Quickly but slyly
the snowflakes creep,
covering the ground
as the earth goes to sleep.
They rest there all winter
not making a sound,
waiting for sunshine
to awaken the ground.

Allison Arnold

Photo Opposite
SQUARE BUTTE, AZ
Gary Ladd

Mrs. Helen Harrington

Helen Harrington, a native of Lamoni, Iowa, has written nearly 10,000 poems in her seventy-seven years. Her material has appeared in such publications as the *Saturday Evening Post*, the *New York Times*, *Good Housekeeping*, and the *Ladies Home Journal*. *Ideals* discovered her poetic talent in 1953, and since then she has been an inspiration to many of our readers.

"Almost everything, really, is interesting to me," said Mrs. Harrington. Her interests are as diversified as farming and tractor-driving, horseback riding and dogs, politics and religion. She possesses a deep interest in people, their philosophies, and world affairs.

This multi-faceted woman attributes her poetic heritage to her parents who loved Tennyson and Byron. Her gift of rhyme was nurtured by excellent teachers and a good library. The "beautiful Iowa-Missouri scenery of trees and fields" inspired her to compose many of her works.

We are proud to feature this small sampling of the poetry of Helen Harrington, *Ideals* Best-Loved Poet.

The Little Gift

God loves the little gift: the widow's mite,
The child's penny, the offering of the poor
Made to the poor. These are his delight.
Subsidies and dowries may ensure
His tabernacle and his singing spire,
His altar and his cloister and his shrine;
But he who gives an alm has strung the lyre
For angels and has built the throne divine.

God likes the flavor of the beggar's crust
Shared with him, the brave and sweet spendthrift
Squandering of self in simple trust—
God loves the little gift.

And it may be, he loves it best of all,
Remembering the gift he gave was small.

Making Christmas

A woman makes Christmas of many things—
A bold red date on the calendar; spruces
And stockings, stickers and strings;
Church choirs, candles, a large bright
Star; and a heart that steadily sings.

A woman makes Christmas by cookies and
Pies, pan and oven. She compiles
Festivity of snowy skies, fires and apples,
And a child's wondering, expectant eyes.

"Peace, goodwill," the angels' sweet song,
She carries in her heart for friends and
For strangers she may meet. And with her
Wish, makes Christmas start in her house
And along her street.

Country Christmas

The country keeps Christmas with quietness, drifting
Snow over hills and through valleys, lifting
Above the woodland, moon and star
To shine down where sheep and cattle are
Huddled together in dark humps, sleeping.

While over the hills, the cities are keeping
Christmas with singing and ringing bells;
Through country sky a silence swells
And it is rife with mystic things
Like the pause after angels fold their wings!

The Rocking Chair

What the world needs now is a rocking chair
On the front porch or the back stoop, where
A lassie may rock her dolls to sleep,
Or a lad may dream, or an old man keep
A drowsy tryst with memory,
Or a mother dandle on her knee
A fretful infant. When we lost
The old-time rocking chair, it cost
Us many an hour of reverie,
Many a sage philosophy.

The world, with its headaches in its hands,
Would find the rocker still withstands
Anger, anguish, fear, and worry;
And, creaking musically, has brought
Many a thinker to his thought,
Many a searcher to his quest,
And many a troubled heart to rest.

Christmas Card Weather

The card the winter weather makes
Is sketched with pens of snow,
A host of fine, fast-flying flakes
That greet you as you go.

And blot the fences out and fill
The paths we used to follow
With sudden peaks, an unknown hill,
An unsuspected hollow.

It scrawls its signature on brooks
And crystals it in ice,
And makes a fairyland of nooks
And boughs. And in a trice

Has framed a wish as wide and clear
As is our wish tonight,
For warm, old-fashioned Christmas cheer
And Christmas crisp and white!

Room the Children Know

This is the room the children know—
Not chair and table placed just so,
Not netted curtains, papered walls,
But a room of jungle waterfalls
Where eagles fly, head-hunters work,
Wolf packs howl and lions lurk;

A room where giants live behind
The floor lamp or the window blind;
And ogres hold the bridge-divan
As only hateful ogres can;
A room where Indian, buffalo,
And big black bears are bitter foe;

A world of fierce magic where
Even grown-ups well might "scare"
Till they learn this enchanted place
Is but a challenge children face
And thus grow strong, against the day
The lions will not fade away!

Lighted Window

Cutting through the woods at evening,
All the trees stood still and white;
With the snow-filled hollows gleaming,
Moonlight threaded through the night!
And the hush upon the hours
Settled like a cloak of gray,
Which I drew about my shoulders
As I went upon my way.

The midnight skies were crowded
With starflowers, sliver thin,
And upon my brow the muted
Benediction of the wind!
The thoughts that sped before me
Matched the winged ones close behind;
The barriers were lifted as
Peace placed her hand in mine!

I passed a neighbor's cottage
As I started up the hill,
Where the soft glow from a candle
Fell across his windowsill.
And its warmth remained within me
As I marvelled at the sight
Of one small penny candle,
That lit a winter night!

Grace E. Easley

Photo Opposite
SNOWBOUND
Dick Smith

"To Our Readers..."

What shall I wish you for Christmas,
This season of joy and delight,
The sound of carol songsters
On a starlit Christmas night?

What can I wish you for Christmas?
What is the thing you desire?
Is it health, wealth, or happiness,
Or the warmth of a Christmas fire?

What can I wish you for Christmas
To give all the joy I am able—
A merry time with good, true friends
Around the fare of a Christmas table?

So much I would wish you for Christmas,
Yet only my greetings I send,
For all that I have to offer
Is the sincere heart of a friend.

Olive Miller

Please accept my sentiments
At this time of year
For a Merry Christmas
Full of hope and cheer.

I would wish you gladness, too,
To lodge within your heart,
And the spirit of Christmas
A new peace to impart.

I would wish you ample parts
Of good health and cheer,
Adequate enough to last you
Through another year.

May your path be paved with stars—
A new light your way wend;
I would wish God's best for you;
Merry Christmas, my friend!

Georgia B. Adams

ACKNOWLEDGMENTS

THE CHRISTMAS ASSEMBLY from *A MONTH OF MONDAYS* by Mary Lou Carney. Copyright © 1984 by Abingdon Press. Used by permission. MARY OF NAZARETH from *HEART CRIES* by Mary Lou Carney. Copyright © 1986 by Abingdon Press. Used by permission. Our sincere thanks to the following whose addresses we were unable to locate: Esther Boomer Baker for THINKING OF YOU AT CHRISTMAS; Virginia Brasier for THE EVERGREEN SCENT; Grace E. Easley for LIGHTED WINDOW; Phyllis M. Flaig for PERFECT GIFT; Leigh Hanes for SANTA CLAUS; Helen Ireland Hays for CHRISTMAS EVE; Alice B. Johnson for WHEN YOU WERE ONLY TWO; Roy Z. Kemp for JOYOUS SEASON; Vera E. Maddry for WINTER MAGIC from her book *WHISPERINGS,* copyright © 1951; the estate of Elizabeth Lathrop Powers for ICE ETCHINGS; Sophia P. Snow for ANNIE AND WILLIE'S PRAYER.

ADDITIONAL PHOTOGRAPH ACKNOWLEDGMENT
Page 80 from Hampfler Studios

Inside back cover , WINTER FOREST, by Ed Cooper

MERRY CHRISTMAS
from all of us at *ideals*